ARIZONA CARDINALS

BY ANDRES YBARRA

SportsZone
An Imprint of Abdo Publishing
abdopublishing.com

abdopublishing.com

Published by Abdo Publishing, a division of ABDO, PO Box 398166, Minneapolis, Minnesota 55439. Copyright © 2017 by Abdo Consulting Group, Inc. International copyrights reserved in all countries. No part of this book may be reproduced in any form without written permission from the publisher. SportsZone™ is a trademark and logo of Abdo Publishing.

Printed in the United States of America, North Mankato, Minnesota
042016
092016

THIS BOOK CONTAINS RECYCLED MATERIALS

Cover Photo: Greg Trott/AP Images
Interior Photos: Greg Trott/AP Images, 1, 26; Gene J. Puskar/AP Images 4-5; Ross D. Franklin/AP Images, 6; Charlie Riedel/AP Images, 7; Scott Boehm/AP Images, 8-9; AP Images, 10-11, 14-15; Bettmann/Corbis, 12-13; Pro Football Hall of Fame/AP Images, 16, 17; NFL Photos/AP Images, 18, 20-21, 22-23; Tony Tomsic/AP Images, 19; Rob Schumacher/AP Images, 24-25; Roy Dabner/AP Images, 27; Ric Tapia/AP Images, 28-29

Editor: Patrick Donnelly
Series Designer: Nikki Farinella

Cataloging-in-Publication Data
Names: Ybarra, Andres, author.
Title: Arizona Cardinals / by Andres Ybarra.
Description: Minneapolis, MN : Abdo Publishing, [2017] | Series: NFL up close | Includes index.
Identifiers: LCCN 2015960327 | ISBN 9781680782066 (lib. bdg.) | ISBN 9781680776171 (ebook)
Subjects: LCSH: Arizona Cardinals (Football team)--History--Juvenile literature.
 | National Football League--Juvenile literature. | Football--Juvenile literature.
 | Professional sports--Juvenile literature. | Football teams--Arizona--Juvenile literature.
Classification: DDC 796.332--dc23
LC record available at http://lccn.loc.gov/2015960327

TABLE OF CONTENTS

OH, SO CLOSE 4

EARLY DAYS 10

CHAMPS AND A CHANGE 14

ST. LOUIS BLUES 18

ON TO THE DESERT 24

Timeline 30
Glossary 31
Index / About the Author 32

OH, SO CLOSE

The Arizona Cardinals were in a tough spot. They had enjoyed a great 2008 season. They had reached the Super Bowl for the first time. But with the clock ticking down, the Cardinals' backs were against the wall. Arizona had the ball at its own 36-yard line. Less than three minutes remained, and the Pittsburgh Steelers were leading 20-16.

Cardinals quarterback Kurt Warner barks out signals against the Pittsburgh Steelers in the Super Bowl.

Quarterback Kurt Warner threw a pass to Larry Fitzgerald. The talented wide receiver made the catch and broke away from three defenders. Fitzgerald raced 64 yards for a touchdown. The Cardinals led 23-20 and were on the verge of their first Super Bowl win.

Wide receiver Larry Fitzgerald caught a 64-yard touchdown pass from Kurt Warner in the Super Bowl.

Larry Fitzgerald celebrates his go-ahead touchdown against the Pittsburgh Steelers in the Super Bowl.

FAST FACT
In 2013, Larry Fitzgerald became the youngest player in NFL history to reach 11,000 career receiving yards.

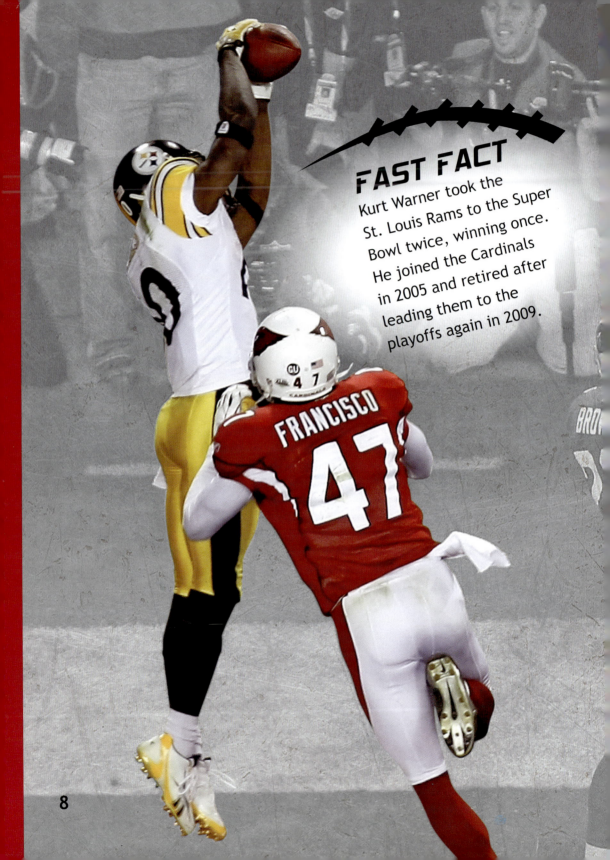

FAST FACT

Kurt Warner took the St. Louis Rams to the Super Bowl twice, winning once. He joined the Cardinals in 2005 and retired after leading them to the playoffs again in 2009.

The Cardinals defense took the field. Pittsburgh would have to go 78 yards to score a touchdown. But Arizona could do little to stop the Steelers. They moved down the field quickly. Finally, Steelers wide receiver Santonio Holmes caught a short pass in the corner of the end zone. He barely got his toes in bounds. But it was enough. The Steelers had come back to win one of the most exciting Super Bowls of all time.

Cardinals safety Aaron Francisco, *47*, can not keep Santonio Holmes from getting his feet down in the end zone on the Steelers' game-winning touchdown.

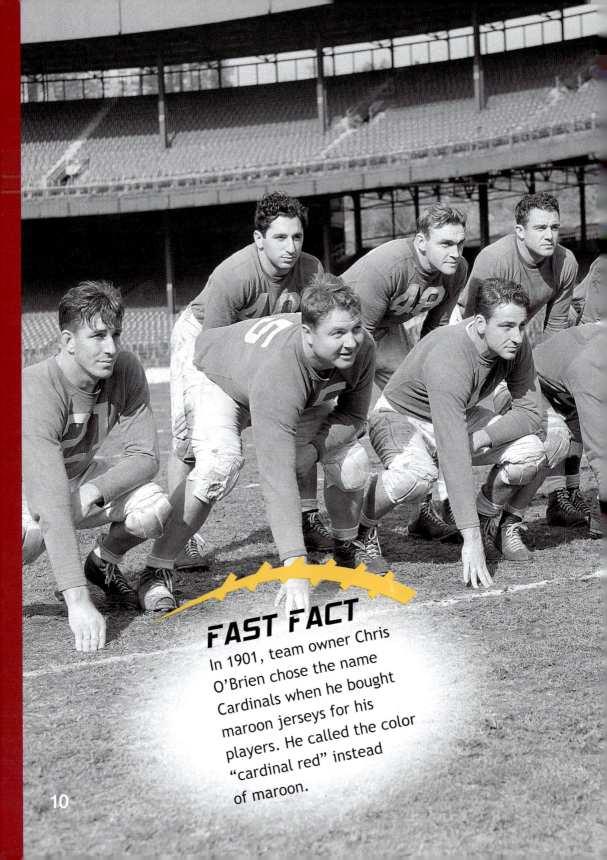

FAST FACT

In 1901, team owner Chris O'Brien chose the name Cardinals when he bought maroon jerseys for his players. He called the color "cardinal red" instead of maroon.

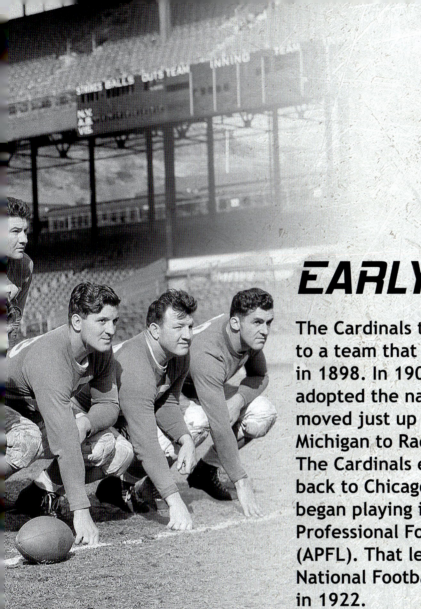

EARLY DAYS

The Cardinals trace their roots to a team that began in Chicago in 1898. In 1901, the team adopted the name Cardinals and moved just up the coast of Lake Michigan to Racine, Wisconsin. The Cardinals eventually moved back to Chicago, where they began playing in the American Professional Football League (APFL). That league became the National Football League (NFL) in 1922.

Members of the 1939 Chicago Cardinals pose for a photo at the Polo Grounds in New York.

Back in Chicago, the Cardinals played their home games at Comiskey Park, home of baseball's Chicago White Sox. They won their first NFL title in 1925. That was before the NFL used playoffs to determine a champion. The Cardinals finished with the league's best record at 11-2-1.

There were down years, too. So many NFL players fought in World War II (1939-1945) that some teams had to combine to have enough players. In 1944, the Cardinals and the Pittsburgh Steelers joined forces. The team was called Card-Pitt and finished the season 0-10.

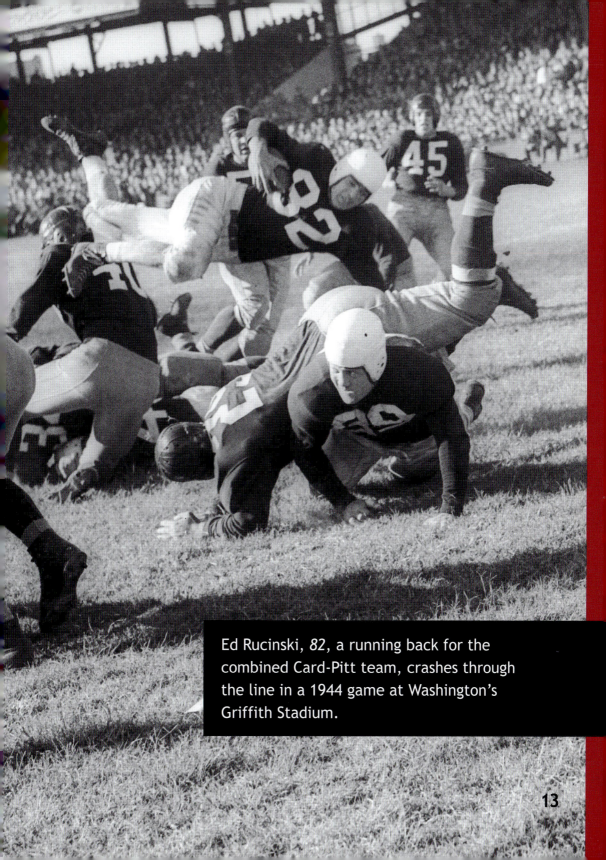

Ed Rucinski, *82*, a running back for the combined Card-Pitt team, crashes through the line in a 1944 game at Washington's Griffith Stadium.

CHAMPS AND A CHANGE

In 1947, the Cardinals won their first NFL Western Division title. They clinched it with a 30-21 win over their crosstown rivals, the Chicago Bears.

Next, they hosted the Philadelphia Eagles in their first NFL Championship Game. The Cardinals relied on a handful of big plays. Halfback Elmer Angsman had two 70-yard touchdown runs. Teammate Charley Trippi scored on a 44-yard run and a 75-yard punt return. It was enough to beat the Eagles 28-21.

FAST FACT

The Bears and the Cardinals represent the NFL's oldest rivalry. The teams started playing against each other in 1920 as the Racine Cardinals and the Decatur Staleys.

Cardinals coach Jimmy Conzelman, *center*, celebrates with running backs Elmer Angsman, *left*, and Charley Trippi after winning the 1947 NFL title.

The Cardinals were even better in 1948. They rolled to an 11-1 record and again beat the Bears in the final game of the season to win the West Division. They faced the Eagles again in a championship game rematch. A blizzard hit Philadelphia that day. Both offenses struggled in the snow. The Eagles scored in the fourth quarter to win 7-0.

That started a string of tough years for the Cardinals. They had only two winning seasons of their next 11. In 1960, team owners decided to move the Cardinals from Chicago to St. Louis.

Cardinals linebacker Corwin Clatt, 67, and defensive back John Cochran, 24, close in on Eagles running back Steve Van Buren during the 1948 NFL Championship Game in snowy Philadelphia.

Hall of Fame running back Ernie Nevers in 1930

FAST FACT
Ernie Nevers scored six touchdowns and kicked four extra points as the Cardinals beat the Bears 40-0 in 1929. No other NFL player has ever scored 40 points in a game.

ST. LOUIS BLUES

St. Louis is known as a baseball town. Its baseball team—also named the Cardinals—has dominated the local sports scene for decades. An NFL team had never lasted more than a year there. The "football Cardinals," as they were often called, struggled to get a foothold in their new town. But they had a few highlights along the way.

Hall of Fame safety Larry Wilson intercepted 52 passes in his 13-year career with the St. Louis Cardinals.

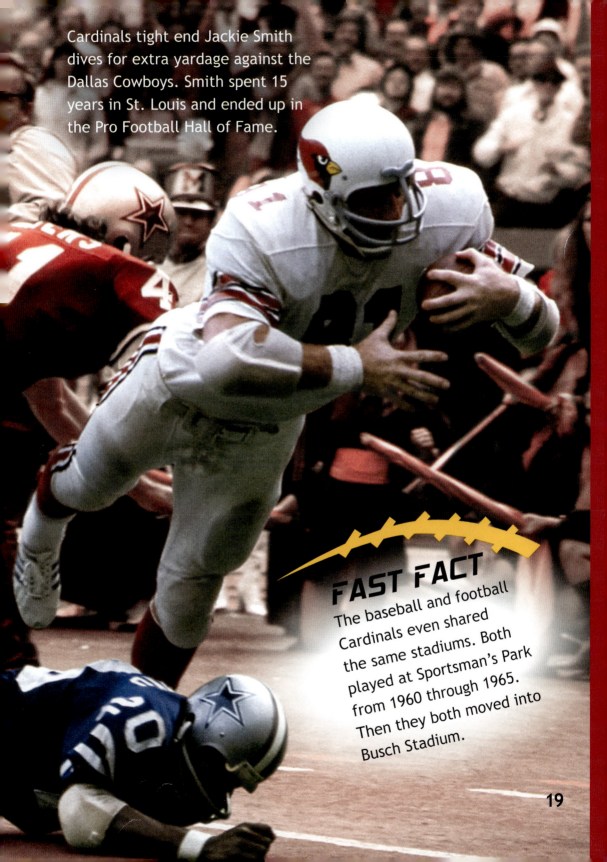

Cardinals tight end Jackie Smith dives for extra yardage against the Dallas Cowboys. Smith spent 15 years in St. Louis and ended up in the Pro Football Hall of Fame.

FAST FACT

The baseball and football Cardinals even shared the same stadiums. Both played at Sportsman's Park from 1960 through 1965. Then they both moved into Busch Stadium.

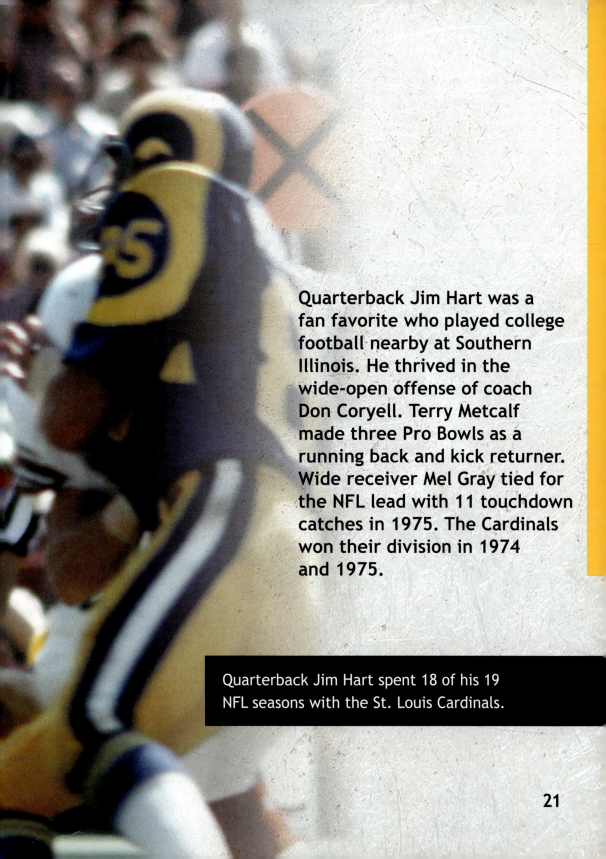

Quarterback Jim Hart was a fan favorite who played college football nearby at Southern Illinois. He thrived in the wide-open offense of coach Don Coryell. Terry Metcalf made three Pro Bowls as a running back and kick returner. Wide receiver Mel Gray tied for the NFL lead with 11 touchdown catches in 1975. The Cardinals won their division in 1974 and 1975.

Quarterback Jim Hart spent 18 of his 19 NFL seasons with the St. Louis Cardinals.

But the Cardinals sputtered in the playoffs both years, losing to the Minnesota Vikings and Los Angeles Rams. They returned to the playoffs in 1982 but lost again in the first round. Fan support slipped, and attendance dropped. After the 1987 season, the team's owners decided they needed a change. The Cardinals packed up and headed to the desert.

Terry Metcalf, *21*, looks for running room in a 1975 NFL playoff game against the Los Angeles Rams.

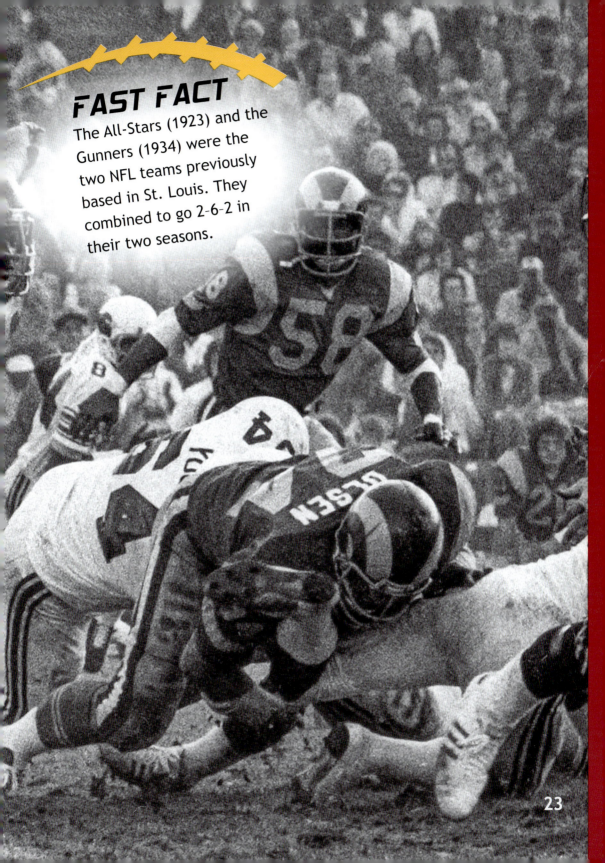

FAST FACT

The All-Stars (1923) and the Gunners (1934) were the two NFL teams previously based in St. Louis. They combined to go 2-6-2 in their two seasons.

ON TO THE DESERT

Fans in Phoenix greeted the Cardinals warmly in 1988. More than 67,000 people attended their first home game. They played the Dallas Cowboys on a Monday night at Arizona State's Sun Devil Stadium.

The Cardinals had a record of 7-4 in mid-November and the playoffs were in their sights. But they ended the season on a five-game losing streak, a sign of more frustrations to come.

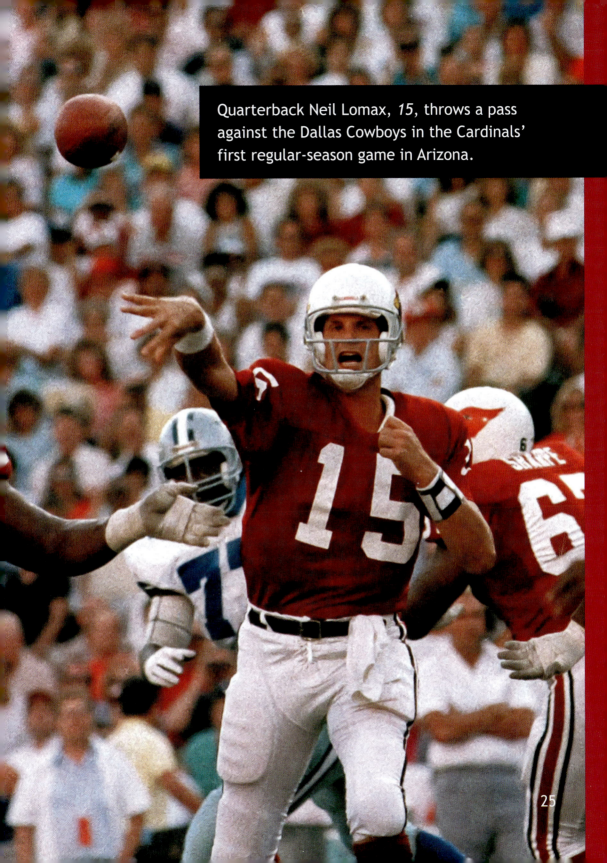

Quarterback Neil Lomax, *15*, throws a pass against the Dallas Cowboys in the Cardinals' first regular-season game in Arizona.

The Cardinals did not have a winning season in their first 10 years in Arizona. Then in 1998, quarterback Jake Plummer led them to a 9-7 record and a wild-card spot in the playoffs. They won their first postseason game in 51 years, beating the Cowboys 20-7 in Dallas. But it took another decade before they returned to the playoffs.

Quarterback Jake Plummer led the Cardinals to the playoffs in 1998.

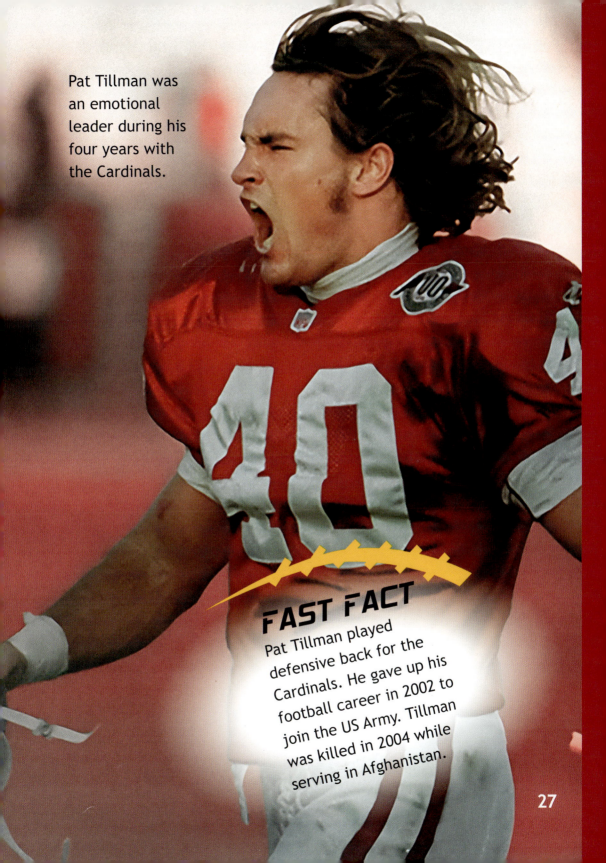

Pat Tillman was an emotional leader during his four years with the Cardinals.

FAST FACT

Pat Tillman played defensive back for the Cardinals. He gave up his football career in 2002 to join the US Army. Tillman was killed in 2004 while serving in Afghanistan.

FAST FACT
The Cardinals moved into University of Phoenix Stadium in 2006. The domed stadium can seat more than 72,000 people.

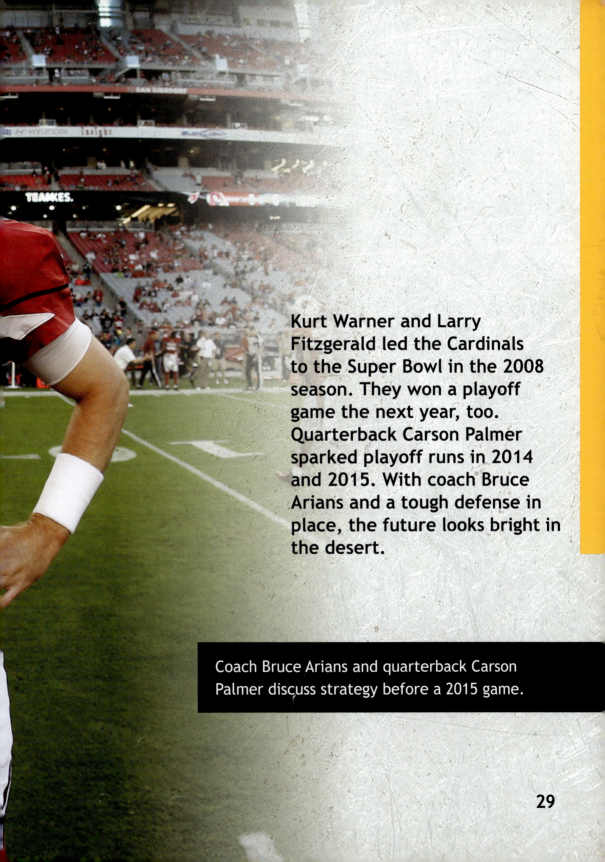

Kurt Warner and Larry Fitzgerald led the Cardinals to the Super Bowl in the 2008 season. They won a playoff game the next year, too. Quarterback Carson Palmer sparked playoff runs in 2014 and 2015. With coach Bruce Arians and a tough defense in place, the future looks bright in the desert.

Coach Bruce Arians and quarterback Carson Palmer discuss strategy before a 2015 game.

TIMELINE

1920
The Racine Cardinals become one of 11 charter members of the APFL.

1922
The team moves to its new home in Chicago's Comiskey Park.

1925
The Cardinals finish with the best record in the NFL to win their first league championship.

1947
The Cardinals beat the Philadelphia Eagles 28-21 in the NFL Championship Game.

1948
The Eagles win a title game rematch, beating the Cardinals 7-0 in a blizzard in Philadelphia.

1960
The Cardinals move from Chicago to St. Louis.

1988
After just three playoff appearances in 28 years in St. Louis, the Cardinals move to Phoenix, Arizona.

1999
On January 2, the Arizona Cardinals beat the Dallas Cowboys for their first playoff win since 1947.

2006
University of Phoenix Stadium opens.

2009
On February 1, the Cardinals play in their first Super Bowl, losing to the Pittsburgh Steelers 27-23.

GLOSSARY

ADOPT
To choose or take on.

CLINCH
To make something certain or final.

FOOTHOLD
A position that makes it possible to begin an activity or effort.

PLAYOFFS
A set of games after the regular season that decides which team will be the champion.

RETIRE
To withdraw from a job or occupation.

RIVAL
An opponent with whom a player or team has a fierce and ongoing competition.

ROOTS
The cause or source of something.

INDEX

Angsman, Elmer, 14, 15
Arians, Bruce, 29
Clatt, Corwin, 16
Cochran, John, 16
Conzelman, Jimmy, 15
Coryell, Don, 21
Fitzgerald, Larry, 6, 7, 29
Francisco, Aaron, 9
Gray, Mel, 21
Hart, Jim, 21
Holmes, Santonio, 9
Lomax, Neil, 25
Metcalf, Terry, 21, 22
Nevers, Ernie, 17
O'Brien, Chris, 10
Palmer, Carson, 29
Plummer, Jake, 26
Rucinski, Ed, 13
Smith, Jackie, 19
Southern Illinois University, 21
Tillman, Pat, 27
Trippi, Charley, 14, 15
Van Buren, Steve, 16
Warner, Kurt, 4, 6, 8, 29
Wilson, Larry, 18
World War II, 12

ABOUT THE AUTHOR

Andres (Andy) Ybarra is a public relations executive and freelance sports writer. He has covered the Minnesota Vikings, Twins, Timberwolves, Wild, and University of Minnesota athletics. He lives in the Twin Cities with his wife and three children.